Singing Like a Cricket, Hooting Like an Owl

Singing Like a Cricket, Hooting Like an Owl

*Selected Poems
of Yi Kyu-bo*

Translated by
Kevin O'Rourke

Cornell East Asia Program
Cornell University
Ithaca, New York 14853

The Cornell East Asia Series is published by the Cornell University East Asia Program and is not affiliated with Cornell University Press. We are a small, non-profit press, publishing reasonably priced books on a wide variety of scholarly topics relating to East Asia as a service to the academic community and the general public. We accept standing orders which may be cancelled at any time and which provide for automatic billing and shipping of each title in the series upon publication.

If after review by internal and external readers a manuscript is accepted for publication, it is published on the basis of camera-ready copy provided by the volume author. Each author is thus responsible for any necessary copy-editing and for manuscript formatting. Submission inquiries should be addressed to Editorial Board, East Asia Program, Cornell University, Ithaca, New York 14853-7601.

Publication of this book was supported by a generous grant from the Korean Culture and Arts Foundation.

Contents

vi

his guests to chortle with glee. We drank three or four cups. Things
quieted down and we had a lovely time. I don't suppose I'll ever have
quite so entertaining a night again, so I thought I'd commemorate
the occasion with a poem, 49

viii

Introduction

Yi Kyu-bo (1168-1241) was born into a very turbulent period of Korean history: all through his life the Koryo kingdom was threatened to the north by barbarian tribes and from within by the on-going struggle for power between the civil and military factions in the bureaucracy. Three times he failed the civil service examination before finally succeeding in 1189. His failures were not due to any lack of ability—he was already recognised as a child prodigy—but rather to a penchant for too much wine and song and too little formal study. Even after passing the civil service examination, he spent many years outside the bureaucracy before a chance meeting with General Ch'oe Chung-hon led to recognition of his ability and consequent preferment, whereupon he had a long and distinguished public career.

Yi Kyu-bo is the Korean poet of transcendence. Some point to his personal ambition, others point to his over-indulgence in wine and his failure to devote himself to bureaucratic tasks as chinks in the armor of a poet of transcendence. Yi Kyu-bo's distinction lies, however, not in any claims to personal transcendence, which in any event would be an arrogance, but in his ability to perceive transcendence in others and to bemoan his own lack of it. A kinder generation would call it humility.

Yi Kyu-bo's poems are *hanshi*, that is, poems in Chinese characters following all the rules of Chinese prosody, but written by Korean poets. The enormity of Yi Kyu-bo's achievement becomes apparent when one considers that Korean and Chinese do not belong to the same language family. Korean, in fact, is as different from Chinese as English is from Korean. A Korean poet writing Chinese poetry attempts the equivalent of a Chinese poet writing classical Latin poetry. Small wonder if many of the Korean *hanshi* poets did not meet the standard! The wonder of Yi Kyu-bo is that he did.

When we think of Chinese poetry, and indeed *hanshi*, we tend to think of moonlight on the autumn river; flower petals in the yard; travelling scholars with lame donkeys, usually looking for a winehouse to make a stop; lonely mountain temples with sage monks; or nobleman types sporting in bamboo groves and pine pavilions. Our perception is that of an extremely romantic tradition, far removed from the everyday cares of this world. The tradition at its best is quite different: so far from being sugary and vapid, Yi Kyu-bo's poems are vibrantly alive, solidly grounded in the cares and concerns of everyday life. Focused on an emotion, they offer brief but brilliant illuminations of the heart.

The texts are from *Tongggukisanggukchonjip*. I am indebted to many Korean friends for help in interpreting the texts and shaping the translations.

On the road: hearing the sounds
of paduk stones in a pavilion

Behind the bamboo curtain shadows are indistinct;
paduk stones rattle across the board like hail
after rain has cleared.
Skill, great or little, is irrelevant here;
the pleasure is in the clinking of the stones.

Note: Paduk stones are the pieces used in the game of Go.

Farmhouse: three poems

The village mill echoes
    through wispy smoke crisscrosses.
There are no walls along the length of the lane;
    clustered thorny trees are demarcators here.
Horses dot the mountain;
    cattle are scattered through the fields.
Everywhere I see the face
    of a great age of peace.

The loom importunes
    in the heavy frost and chill of dawn.
In the darkening smoke of the setting sun,
    the woodcutter sings as he returns.
How could an old countryman know
    the ninth day of the ninth month?
Yet he dips in his mellow wine
    those yellow chrysanthemums he chanced upon.

The leaves of the mountain pear are red;
    yellow the leaves of the mulberry.
Along the road the breeze returns,
    thick with the fragrance of rice stalks.
The sound of water being scooped from the well
    is echoed in the wooden clogs;
through the open brushwood gate,
    moonlight carpets the frost.

2

Song of the paulownia

Shade once a broad thick curtain,
now swirling leaves scatter like beads.
Planted originally for the noble phoenix,
a ragged motley nests here now.

Cool spring

For dry travellers, north and south,
there's a cool spring by the roadside.
One small spring gives abundance to the land;
bow twice before you drink.

Big tree

Good for relief from dog-day heat;
perfect for refuge from sudden summer showers;
an umbrella of cool shade;
purveyor of benefits various.

Poetry: a chronic disease

I'm over seventy now,
an official of the first rank;
I know I should give up writing poetry,
but somehow I can't.
Mornings I sing like a cricket;
evenings I hoot like an owl.
I'm possessed by a devil I can't exorcise;
night and day it follows me stealthily around.
Once possessed, there's never a moment free;
a pretty mess it's got me in.
Day after day, I shrivel heart and liver
just to write a few poems.
Body fats and fluids depleted,
there's nothing left but skin and grizzle.
Bones protruding, struggling to recite,
I strike a very foolish figure.
I have no words to elicit wonder,
nothing to pass on that will last a thousand years.
I clap my hands, guffaw, and when the laughter
        bout subsides, I begin to recite again.
My life and death hang on poetry;
not even a physician could cure this disease.

Drinking cold wine with a guest
one winter's day:
composed playfully

Snow fills the capital;
  the price of charcoal has soared.
Cold bottle, frozen hands;
  the fragrant *makkolli* is poured.
Don't you know how wine in the belly
  soon generates its own heat;
I suggest you wait for the rose afterglow
  to come into your cheeks.

The secretary got a beautiful kisaeng
to bring me paper and request a poem;
my brush flew and I presented this.

The heart of the man becomes the heart of a girl;
in the moment of parting, tears fondly sprinkle my collar.
The wayfarer's bag is empty; it holds nothing fine.
I'll give you a poem; it's worth a thousand gold coins.

Rhyming with Old Mun's improvisation on
"Meeting along the Road"

Two men, at their ease—they have neither post nor temple—
meet along the road. They clasp and clasp each other's hand.
Who can know the depth of meaning of that handshake?
They stand upon the dusty road, wordless in the setting sun.

Makkolli song

In the old wandering, carefree days
makkolli was my regular drink,
and if, on occasion, I got clear wine,
I couldn't resist the glow of a binge.
But when I rose to high station,
there was no reason to have makkolli.
Now old and retired, my stipend reduced,
the rice bin is often empty.
Good wine is a commodity that comes and goes,
and makkolli occasions are starting to grow.
Makkolli lies on the stomach; it clogs the digestion;
now I know the evils of cheap wine.
Tu Fu claimed, though I didn't understand at the time,
that makkolli was a receptacle of the sublime.
I understand now:
personality is colored by living standards;
food follows status;
how could likes and dislikes be of consequence?
Thus I tell my wife to be frugal with what goes out,
no matter how much is coming in,
and when she fills the wine-jar, I tell her
not to fill it with water-clear wine.

Visit to the hermitage of Master Ka,
using a rhyme written on the wall
by someone long dead

Desolate the monk's room beside an ancient tree;
One lamp, one incense burner in the shrine.
No need to ask the old monk how he spends his days?
A chat when a guest comes; when he goes, a nap.

Visited the Temple of Many Blessings
on the ninth day of the ninth month:
the abbot fed me wine and made me stay

No white clad servant in front of the door;
I proceeded alone to the monks' quarters
    and looked for wine.
Garlands festooned my head, fragrance filled my mouth;
no need to moan that the yellow chrysanthemum
    had bloomed in vain.

Rhyming with the invitation of Monk Chongui from Heavenly Life Temple

Five months since we met.
Your invitation came out of the blue:
    soon I'm mounted and on my way.
My worn-out donkey is unaware of the urgency of my quest:
it stoops to drink at every stream I meet.

Self derision

My shoulders are cold, the bones stick up;
my hair is diseased, stubbly and sparse as mugworth.
Who said I was to be the last of the honest men,
that I shouldn't fold and unfold with the times?
When deceit is rampant, there are tigers in the marketplace;
when justice reigns, there are no fish in the water.
Perhaps it's best if I become an old farmer,
go back to the plough and daily carry the hoe.

Resting at Shihu Inn

Excessive thirst is an old complaint.
Muggy summer's day; I set out again on a long journey.
With a pot of tea I try an experiment in taste;
it's like frozen snow going down my throat.
I rest again awhile in the pine pavilion;
already I feel autumn in every bone.
The lad can't understand me at all;
he thinks it weird I delay so long.
My disposition has always been broad and liberal:
when I get to a place, I stay as long as I want;
when I meet an obstruction, immediately I stop;
when I ride a river, immediately I float.
What's the harm in staying here?
What's in it for me, if I go over there?
There's a lot of space between sky and earth;
my life has tranquility.

15

Winter night: small party
in a mountain temple

Banquets in warm rooms are nightly affairs
in the houses of the great.
Riches and honor, however, easily lose their savor.
Nothing's better than the glow of makkolli warmed
leisurely in the embers
in my mountain study late on a snowy night.

Reading T'ao Yuan-ming's poems

I love T'ao Yuan-ming;
his poems are limpid and pure.
He always strummed a stringless lyre;
his poems have that same quiet grace.
Sublime rhythm is of its nature soundless;
there's no need to strum the lyre.
Sublime language is of its nature worldless;
it's not necessary to carve and trim.
This is a wisdom that springs from nature,
the longer chewed the better the taste.
T'ao Yuan-Ming freed himself from official business:
        he returned to the country,
to wander among pine, bamboo and chrysanthemum.
When he had no wine, he sought out a friend;
he fell down drunk every day.
On the sleeping bench he stretched his body out;
the breeze blew cool and refreshing.
From the bright ancient world he came,
a scholar noble and true.
I think of the man when I read the poems;
his integrity will be praised for a thousand years.

Presented playfully to Kim Chongon
after I received the robe of Sagan (1)

Of old when I wore a blue jacket,
    people didn't really avoid me,
but now that I have donned purple robes,
    a bickering throng follows me around.
My face and rank are as they were of old,
the only difference is my clothes.

Note: Sagan and Chongon are both 6th rank posts.

Presented playfully to Kim Chongon
after I received the robe of Sagan (2)

I've taken off green and put on purple;
yet my white locks and black face
    are just as they've always been.
The jade belt girding my waist
    weighs me down with responsibility.
From tonight I'd better keep my eyes open
    and sleep less.

Presented to Chon I-ji on a visit:
we drank together and got terribly drunk

A close friend came on a visit:
my circumstances, however, were so straightened
      I couldn't buy wine.
He sat down, leisure written on his face:
I knew we couldn't spend the whole day in talk.
So I pawned the old rags on my back,
exchanging them for a jar of clear brimming wine.
Cup after cup we tilted till the wine joy came on us;
we seemed to gallop like crazy horses
      loosed from the bridle.
My songs shook the trees in the forest;
his brush made the river reverse its current.
My songs grew coarse as if washing away resentment;
his brush sped with cruel intent as if discharging anger.
Who was wise and who was foolish,
who had gained and who had lost?
The man who gained was not necessarily wise;
the covetous and the mean rise to high station.
The man who lost was not necessarily foolish;
the illustrious in thought and deed live in poverty.
Forget about me—I'm insignificant—but my friend,
a great man, a hero, why has he no official rank?
Rogues rise up while good men stay stuck to the ground.
The crooked seize their opportunity;
the straight are put to rout.
Discussing the affairs of a lifetime with you,

19

I spat out in wine things that always weighed me down.
By turns I caressed my long-sword, danced,
        sat and drank again,
a cup, then another and another . . .

I hate flies when I'm trying to sleep

Shew them off, back they come again; energy flags.
I cover myself with the quilt and try to sleep,
      but dreams prove elusive.
Why blame these persecutors of the body:
they fly to their death in wine glasses
      and don't even know it?

Who else would so covet the smell of meat?
They stipple everything, black and white.
What's in the dreary bedclothes
that they band together to buzz me
when I'm trying to sleep?

The mad rout of the rat

My reason for raising a cat was not to catch you;
I had hoped that the sight of the cat
    would make you cower and hide.
But you don't hide;
instead you bore through the walls,
    you come and go at will: why, why?
It's bad enough that you come out to play;
how dare you instigate this present mad rout!
Your squabbles are so raucous you interfere with sleep;
you steal our food with incredible speed.
The fact that you whizz around in spite of the cat
shows that the cat is lacking in skill.
The cat may not be doing its job,
but your crimes are weighty still.
I can whip the cat, I can drive it out,
but you are difficult to catch and tie.
Rats, rats, mend your ways
or I'll govern you with a fierce new cat.

Song of an incident that occurred
in the K'aiyuan-T'ienpao era:
cutting the hair

Excessive love turned to rancor,
often, and with intent, the queen in word
        provoked the king to anger.
But why should she be bitter?
        She got the royal summons to return:
her hair was more than enough
        to buy the king's favor again.

Note: Queen Yang of T'ang, the Cleopatra of the Orient, wanted more attention from her husband, so she feigned a love interest in one of the generals. The king was enraged and sent her home, but the queen in token of her love sent the king a tress of her cloud black hair, the only thing of value she possessed that the king had not given her, whereupon the king overcome again by his love sent for her to return.

23

Sea Rose

Sea rose, head drooped in heavy sleep,
like Queen Yang after a lot of wine:
wakened from dreams by the oriole's song,
smiling, allurement is on your mind.

Thinking of my children:
first of two poems

I have a young daughter;
already she knows how to call her dad and mom.
She drags her skirt along and plays at my knees;
she takes the mirror and imitates her mother at make-up.
How many months now since we parted?
Suddenly it's as if she were by my side.
By nature I'm a wanderer;
dejected, I live in this foreign place.
For weeks I've been on a binge;
I've been laid up sick for a month.
I turn my head and look toward the palace in Seoul;
mountains and streams stretch oppressively far.
This morning suddenly I thought of you;
tears flowed down, wetting my skirt.
Boy, hurry and feed the horse;
my desire to go home grows more urgent
with every passing day.

Evening on the mountain:
song to the moon in the well (1)

Blue water ripples the well at the corner of the mossy rock.
The new moon is beautifully etched therein.
I scoop out some water but only half a shadow enters my jar.
I fear I'll bring only half the golden mirror home.

Evening on the mountain:
song to the moon in the well (2)

A mountain monk coveted the moon;
he drew water, a whole jar full;
but when he reached his temple, he discovered
that tilting the jar meant spilling the moon.

Written on the upper story
of Yosong Posthouse

When the mood comes, I order a carriage;
    when I feel tired, I rest.
A thousand thanks to heaven and earth
    for freeing me for such leisure.
I feel sorry for the white-haired official
    who works the station;
he's cast an entire life
    between the hooves of a horse.

How I felt pawning my coat: shown to Ch'oe Chong-bon

Third month, eleventh day;
no reason to light the kitchen fire this morning.
The wife said she'd pawn my fur;
I scolded her at first and stopped her.
Suppose the cold has already gone,
what pawnbroker would take the coat?
Suppose the cold returns,
how am I to survive the winter?
The wife retorted angrily:
how can you be so foolish?
I know it's not the most glorious coat ever,
but the thread was woven by these hands;
I grudge it twice as much as you,
but mouth and belly are more urgent than furs.
A man who doesn't eat twice a day, the ancients say,
is heading for starvation,
and a starving man can drop morning or evening;
so how can you promise yourself another winter?
I called the servant and sent him at once to sell the fur.
I thought we'd survive for several days on the proceeds,
but what the servant brought back was no equivalent.
Suspicious, I suggested he might have pocketed some for
          himself.
The servant's face went an angry color.
He quoted the pawnbroker:
already summer encroaches on what's left of spring,
is it reasonable to buy furs at a time like this?
The only reason I'm willing to parry winter early

28

is that I have a little extra.
If I didn't have that bit to spare,
I wouldn't give you a single bag of grain.
Hearing this, I was ashamed, ashamed;
tears flowed down and wet my chin.
Fruit of arduous mid-winter weaving,
given away in a morning,
brings no relief from great hunger;
famished children in a line like bamboo stalks.
I look back to younger more sprightly days
when I knew nothing of the affairs of the world.
For a man who has read thousands of books, I thought,
passing the government examination
will be like pulling a hair from my beard.
I was filled with sudden self-conceit;
surely a good post will be alloted me.
Why have I had such a mediocre lot,
why has poverty embraced my sad path?
Reflecting sincerely on all this,
obviously I'm not without fault.
In my drinking, I never had control;
invariably I tipped a thousand cups.
Words normally kept hidden in my heart
under wine's influence were not kept back.
I didn't stop till I had spewed everything out,
little knowing how false charges and vilification follow.
My conduct uniformly thus,
I deserved all this poverty and hunger.
Those beneath me did not like me,
heaven above denied me its protection.
Wherever I went, things got fouled up;
whatever I did turned out wrong.
All my own doing.
Sad, but who can I blame?
I counted my sins on my fingers
and gave myself three lashes of the whip.
But what's the point in repenting the past;
what I have to do is improve the future.

29

Written on the wall after arriving at Dragon Rock Temple

Here in the flesh at Dragon Rock Temple,
  I wonder if this is where the Immortals live?
With my lips I test Turtle Spring;
  the water tastes like an ice drink.
a thousand pieces of gold would not buy
  the flavor of the monk's house.
Rain falling on the mountain;
  I get myself some sleep.

Summer day happening

I put on my light summer coat
        and lie down on the small bamboo mat
                to catch the breeze on the veranda.
The song of the golden oriole
        interrupts my dream.
Flowers shaded by clustered leaves
        live on when spring has gone;
sunlight filtering through light clouds
        shines brightly in the rain.

One day in the fifth month of the year of Kimi,
a thousand pomegranate flowers bloomed
in Ch'oe Ch'ung-hon's house:
he summoned me to compose a poem

The first flush of wine is on jade faces;
a pink tint invades their world.
Petal folds like fairy wings,
beauty beguiles the guests'souls.
Fresh, fragrant days entice the butterflies;
nights of exploding light awe the birds.
Beauty so prized it's bid bloom late;
who can understand the heart of the Creator?

Burning my manuscripts

In my youth I used to write songs.
When the brush moved down the page,
    I wrote with unimpeded flow.
My poems, I thought, were as beautiful as jade;
who dared talk about flaws?
Afterwards, I studied them again:
there wasn't a fine word in one of them.
To retain them would be to soil my writing box:
unbearable thought, so I burned them in the kitchen fire.
If I look next year at this year's poems,
they will all be the same; I'll scrap them too.
Perhaps that's why Minister Kao of old
first composed when he was fifty.

Cutting down on wine

I'm tired of people branding me a drunkard.
I've cut down lately;
        and of course there are no complaints.
It's just that when I loose my brush
        and try to chant a noble song,
it's as if one wing were broken
        and I cannot spread my plumes.

The governor to the elders

I am an old scholar;
I won't call myself governor.
Thus I present myself to the elders.
Think of me as an old farmer, I say.
If you have a grievance, come and make your case,
like a child looking for mother's milk.
The drought continues; heaven sends no rain;
this, too, is my responsibility.
I apologise sincerely to all the elders.
I think I should resign without delay.
You'll be better off if I go;
where's the point in holding on
          to an old man like me?

The elders reply to the governor

Excellency, your impatience with us
prompts you to resign your post.
Our village land may be barren,
but the natural features
are as strong as a dragon.
Official appointees to the village
receive the royal summons within a matter of months.
We beseech you, excellency, bear with us a while.
Take a rest beneath the sweet pear tree.
An emissary will surely come from the nine gate palace
to escort you to the royal presence.

Note: The reference is to a poem in the Book of Songs. The people of Chou so revered
the memory of Shao Pao's wise government that they treasured an old pear tree under
which he once rested. The people are asking Yi Kyu-bo to be another Shao Pao for
them.

Composed playfully on New Year's Day

This body of mine has lived a lot of years;
I wonder where it has piled them though.
If I could put them in my pocket and count,
I'd empty them out, one by one, and hand them back to Heaven.

Wine and music

Clap hands, roll shoulders, beat time on the thighs;
jumps become dance, cries become song.
This body is an instrument of heavenly delight;
no need to ask for reed pipe or bamboo flute.

Thoughts on eyes growing dim:
presented to Chon I-ji

I'm forty-four now;
both eyes are beginning to blur.
I can't distinguish people even at very close range;
it's as if a dense spring mist were blocking the view.
I consulted a physician. The physician said:
your liver is the problem, it's not what it should be:
or perhaps when you were young,
you read too much in the shadow of the lamp.
Hearing this, I clapped my hands and laughed outright.
You're not a very skilled physician, I said.
People with ears want to hear;
those who can't hear are deaf.
People with eyes want to see;
those who can't see are blind.
I wanted to see the king,
but I had no access to the nine gate palace.
I wanted to see men of rank in ceremonial cloth of gold,
but dressed in hemp I couldn't conceal my presence.
I wanted to see the peonies,
but only useless weeds grew verdant.
I never lived in a first-rate house;
in a hut in a mugworth field my hair turned white.
I never ate fine ceremonial food;
many's the time I missed a meal.
That's why my eyes are dim,
that's why they're bothering me as if veiled in hemp.
This is all the decree of heaven;
I can't cure it with medicine.
Who knows, it may turn out to be a blessing;
I may finish my days deaf and blind.

Composed playfully upon hearing of an errant monk being punished (1)

Long-haired laymen, head-shorn monks,
all who love the flesh share one heart.
Were it not for Buddha's divine power,
a Ma Tung woman would have corrupted Ananda.

Note: The reference is to a woman from the tribe of Ma Tung who tried to seduce the disciple Ananda. Ananda was saved by the merciful intervention of the Buddha.

Composed playfully upon hearing of an errant monk being punished (2)

This monk was lacking in the skills of deception;
    that's why he's been taken in.
The law of the land can't check them all.
Let him rear children; when they're all grown up,
they can be taken to south plain and made to till the fields.

Once again to the rhyme of
"Leasing a Straw Hut"

Better become an old tiller of the soil
than shame myself by buying preferment.
If you live on a government stipend
you're like a monkey in a cage: you eat what you get.
I want to forget the world and fly like a bird.
The deeper you hide jade the more it asserts its beauty;
why should the orchid be sad because it isn't plucked?
My singular joy is to have clusters of black-haired children
running around my sleeping bench.

Tano sentiment: beyond the outer walls

Old tombs, new tombs; next door neighbors.
How many of the occupants spent their lifetimes drunk?
Today their descendants fight to offer a cup.
Can a single drop wet cold lips?

Note: Tano is one of the traditional festivals in the lunar calendar.

Teasing a friend who cannot rise
from wine sickness

I am an old physician skilled in diagnosis.
The culprit here is clearly the god of yeast.
What you must do is toss back five *mal*
of wine at first light,
a prescription handed down from Liu Ling.

Note: Liu Ling was one of the great legendary wine drinkers in ancient China.

Master Un asks for a poem
before returning to the mountains

The world of Bodhi has always taught
       the severing of past and present;
what's all this gloom in the face of parting?
Fear not red dust will follow white feet;
mountain springs gush forth to wash in when you return.

Seventh month, tenth day:
I sang of my feelings at dawn
and showed the poem to Tong Ko-ja

A poet is a man of innate sensibility:
he marvels at autumn in a single leaf,
and though summer heat is still around,
he thinks of warm fur at the approach of dawn.
Yesterday he bathed in south stream;
he swam like a seagull in the water.
Today he looks at those same blue waters;
already cold currents make him baulk.
The seasons change a day at a time;
time never pauses in its flow.
Tomorrow is not today;
black heads change to white.
Life is a brief lodging,
a hundred years at most.
Why be a rat, head stretched out of the hole,
unable to decide on direction?
Small hearts either encompass great pain,
or, harnessing effort to will,
spit on their hands and grab a title.
The alternative is to return to origins,
to sit in the fields and devote oneself to farming.
One hundred measures of wine brewed every year
guarantees old age on wine's hill.
When it comes to death and becoming clay under a pine,
life is the same for low and high.

Reply to the poem of a friend, Yu Chung-gi, using the same rhyme

Your words are weightier than jewels;
I recite and recite them again as I take to the road.
Though great mountains topple,
a strong man's heart never changes.
When fine wine is so plentiful it floats to the sea
and the smiles of beautiful girls are measured in gold,
then you'll understand my resolution;
no need at all for grave warnings now.

Teasing Kim Hoe-yong

There was no pretext to keep you here;
      yet I hated to see you go.
So, I went to the blue pavilion
      and called a gleaming, black chignon.
Another day you'll laugh at this in Seoul:
the impish smile of a beauty
      loosed your saddle home.

One day I lost my way; it was night
when I reached Armpit Village,
where I stayed

About to enter the valley—
    afraid of a hungry tiger;
about to cut through the forest—
    thought I might startle sleeping crows.
Staying in a three-house village;
no need to ask whose house it is!

Having drunk till late, we were taking a short rest, just three or four of us, sitting opposite each other, drinking tea. As it was very late and we had been sitting for a long time, we were tired and our eyes grew heavy. The monk went out and brought back oranges, persimmon and quince for his guests. The drowsiness left me as soon as I began to eat. A little later the monk called the novice, but the novice did not answer; he was fast asleep and snoring. The monk laughed, went into the room and brought out a jar of wine himself, prompting all his guests to chortle with glee. We drank three or four cups. Things quieted down and we had a lovely time. I don't suppose I'll ever have quite so entertaining a night again, so I thought I'd commemorate the occasion with a poem.

Gadding around these last twenty years,
the dust of the world has been my daily diet,
but listening to this night's crystal conversation,
I feel a bracing coolness flowing throughout my body.
The serving table is piled with fruit,
each piece giving off a heavenly fragrance.
How strange that Tung T'ing Lake oranges
have cool juice running through jade flesh.
I am a descendant of I Heng of Wu;
it is fitting that I should savor this taste.
The persimmons have softened and ripened in the frost;
they're so red and shiny they dazzle the eye.
It's gratifying that the eggs of the red dragon
have not been devoured by a flock of crows.
Quince, all pink on one side,
fall, chunk by chunk, to the knife blade.

How can I repay such generous hospitality;
I'm ashamed I have no fine jade.
Coolness remains in the gums and the teeth,
like standing in your home village in the snow.
The pleasurable feelings I've savored tonight
I won't forget for the rest of my life.

Note: When I Heng was governor of Tanyang he planted a thousand orange trees on the shores of Tung T'ing Lake.

Knotweed and herons

The fast water in front abounds with fish;
single-purposed, the herons cleave the waves.
At sight of people they startle and lift;
back they fly to the knotweed rise and regroup.
Necks arched, they wait for the people to go,
fur coats soaked in the fine rain.
Still their hearts are with the fast water fish,
but the people say: they stand there oblivious
of their natural core.

Written on the wall with flying brush,
using once again a rhyme
from one of the ancients

The moon stands out against the gelid blue of sky
    after the rain has cleared.
I can almost hear the raindrops fall
    from the twelve painted lotus blossoms.
There's nothing to do
    except burn incense.
Now at last I realize
    the nobility of the monk's calling.

Thanks to a friend for sending wine

These days the wine cup has run dry;
a drought has stricken this house.
Thanks for your present of fragrant wine;
it's as pleasurable as rain at the proper time.

To a rhyme of Yun Hak-no:
drunk and drowsy at dawn

Sleep town neighbors drunk town;
one body, I pass back and forth between the two.
The ninety days of spring are but a dream
and I am a dreamer within that dream.

Grieving for my little girl

My little girl's face was white as snow;
I can't tell you how bright and intelligent she was.
She was talking by the time she was two,
her tongue more plastic than a parrot.
At three she became girl conscious, reserved;
she didn't go outside the gate to play.
This year she was four; already she was good at sewing.
How could she be deprived of life,
            how could she be gone to the other world?
It was all so sudden it's unreal:
a nestling fallen to the ground before it could grow,
a terrible indictment of her father's home.
I am acquainted with the way;
I can bear my pain to a point,
but the tears of my wife, when will they end?
I look at that field:
new shoots beset by unseasonable wind and hail
face certain destruction.
The Creator put her here;
the Creator just as suddenly snatched her away.
What happens in this world is all subterfuge;
life's comings and goings are illusory.
It's all over now; go in peace to your eternal rest.

Another poem next day

Even when I'm sick
    I can't firmly decline a drink.
The day I die I know will be my first day
    liberated from the cup.
What zest has life
    for a sober man,
but to go to heaven drunk—
    ah, that would be really fine!

More diversion on north mountain

Bow down, look up;
I'm always surprised by the way time flies.
Ten years have passed and I'm still only a student.
I happened on an ancient temple
where I sought vestiges of my former presence.
Suddenly face to face with a ranking monk,
we talked of old affections.
The shadow of a bird flew across
the half wall that caught the evening sun,
and the autumn moon when it filled the mountain
was cold with monkeys' cries.
I have great difficulty in reproducing
the melancholy of fond thoughts;
from time to time I go down into the yard
and walk aimlessly around.

Thinking with longing of O Tok-jon

Clouds stretch ten thousand *li* into the distance;
     my heart is with them.
Tears fall like rain in the empty yard.
Now that you've gone, who have I to talk to?
My eyes hold no new instance of old time blue.

Note: The reference here is to old China: eyes that turned blue (green) to welcome a friend and white to meet an enemy.

Singing again in the boat

Pink fish caught in the fast water,
makkolli bought from the shop on the sands;
little by little I grow close to the old fisherman;
drunk, I lie down in the night rain of the misty river.

Lines on not beating the ox

Don't beat the ox, the ox is to be pitied.
Though the ox be yours, beating it is no imperative.
What wrong has the ox done to you?
Why do you target your abuse at it?
It bears heavy loads long distances;
its shoulders are tired rather than yours.
Its tongue hangs out as it ploughs great fields;
it fills your mouth and your belly.
Having served you so faithfully,
you delight to ride it like a horse.
Fine for you playing the pipe as you ride,
but the jaded ox keeps lagging behind.
The tardier the ox, the more you abuse it,
the more frequently you give it the whip.
Don't beat the ox, the ox is to be pitied.
Should the ox die tomorrow, what would you use?
Cowherd, cowherd, how very foolish;
the ox is not made of iron, how can it endure more?

Drinking beneath the roses in the garden:
presented to Chon I-ji

Last year you came to see me
at the flower planting time.
I shook the muck from my hands;
we began to drink and soon were soused.
This year with the flowers in full bloom
you come from I know not where.
The flowers seem particularly cordial to you;
I wonder was there indebtedness in some former life?
On planting day we raised our cups;
all the more now that the flowers are in bloom.
Do not decline this wine;
you must not disappoint these flowers.

China Rose

I wanted to bloom with spring blossoms,
    but too soon they dropped with the wind.
I wanted to bloom with fall's fragrant crop,
    but this too became an empty dream.
A thorough screening of the flowers around me
    revealed no suitable companion,
so, fresh and lone, I kept
    my red youth for the snow.

Song for the farmer (1)

Bent double in the drills, weeding rice plants in the rain;
face mud-scored, how can I be called human?
Princes of the royal line, do not despise me;
your riches and luxury all stem from me.

Song for the farmer (2)

The new grain is still green in the paddies;
the village clerks have already gathered their taxes.
Ploughed with great effort, the land grows rich;
     all predicated of us.
How can they afflict us so;
     will they take the skin from our bones?

Fish frolic

Red scales shoal on the surface;
    the fish dive and rise again.
Men envy the fish for playing
    to their hearts' content.
But think about it:
    they haven't a moment's rest;
when the fishermen go home,
    the herons come with new intent.

On first entering Yoju:
second of two poems

I packed my bundle in haste:
I traversed a difficult, interminable road.
Burning my beard I tend my sister;
fanning the pillow I recall with longing
    mother's loving face.
Up in the capital the court is dark with wind and dust,
down here in the south the times are leisurely.
This town is well worth settling in;
quite perfect to live in for someone as naive as me.

Note: Li Chi was a high-ranking T'ang official who insisted on personally lighting the fire and preparing the gruel for his ailing sister, a solicitude which once resulted in his beard catching fire. Huang Hsiang from Later Han, who lost his mother at the age of nine, was noted for his filial devotion to his father, in particular, for fanning his father's pillow during the heat of summer.

Song of obliviscence

The people of this world have all forgotten me;
I am alone in the four seas.
It's not just others who have forgotten me,
but my own brothers—they have forgotten me!
Today my wife forgot me;
tomorrow I'll forget myself.
Soon in heaven and earth
I'll have no ties close or distant.

Parting from a beauty

She doesn't ask me when I'll return;
Back and forth she paces;
      unwittingly she grabs my sleeve.
Don't pour your tears
      in a thousand jewelled streams;
make raindrops of them,
      come to me occasionally in dreams.

Coming home drunk from Anhwa-sa Temple

Sozzled drunk in Yoni Pavilion;
I came home at night along the rough stony road.
I went at my leisure, early, alone;
the moon was so bright it brought two of us home.

Went to Wonhung-sa Temple
and visited a monk friend

My mind goes back to the old days
    when we used to go out together in the capital:
I make a calculation; already it's been fourteen years.
You were in your prime physically, not yet thirty;
your body, you claimed, could emulate the wild goose.
I had black glossy hair, the youngest of the group:
my eyes flashed lightning like Wang Jung.
Parting, we dispersed like clouds: no one knew where.
We were like twin mugworth rolling through
the winds and dust of the four seas.
We meet now, have a laugh, caress the copper doll:
tears well, I can't go on, but the heart abides.
My monk friend no longer looks like he did;
he's haggard and gaunt like an old crane on a pine.
I'm old too and my heart has shrivelled;
the rainbow spirit I once had is gone.
We couldn't say everything in our hearts;
in our sorrow neither of us realized
the sun was hanging red half way up the mountain.
Life is but a moment in time;
better forget fame and fortune
    and follow my monk friend, Chigong.

Note: Wang Jung was one of the seven sages of the bamboo forest. Chi Tzu-Hsun from Later Han discovered the secret of becoming one of the Immortals. Rubbing a copper doll, Chi Tzu-Hsun said: "I saw this being made: already it is five hundred years."

Lodging at Miruk Shrine: treated to wine
and side-dishes by a monk I do not know.
          I composed this poem
       and presented it to him in thanks

I took off the bridle and entered the ancient temple,
but I failed to find any way of slaking parched lips.
The shoulders of the poet stuck up like autumn hills;
the *han* of the wanderer fluttered like flags in the wind.
A monk I did not previously know
came out and welcomed me warmly.
The cinnamon wine he poured was blue and fragrant;
the reddish tinge on frosted pears disappeared with peeling.
He alleviated the hunger in Ling Che's famished stomach;
he slaked the thirst in Hsiang Ju's burning throat.
Have you seen, sir, how human bonding works these days?
Relationships are like autumn clouds flying in the wind:
hearts sworn yesterday to adhere like sticky rice cakes
this morning see each other as enemies.
You, sir, still have the old graces;
the name you bear is more famous
          than that of Great Master Hui Yuan.
Today you met a scholar you did not know,
but distance is discounted when minds are one.
From the moment you saw me you treated me as an old friend;
you asked me about the tedium of the wanderer's road.

How can I repay such good will?
I am ashamed to be unable to reciprocate
your kindness with a fine poem.

Note: Han refers to feelings of bitter regret and loss: the han of a nation that loses its sovereignty; the han of a widow; the han of lost love, the han of a mother who loses an only son. Ling Che is a figure of the last stages of starvation. Hsiang Ju had a sickness which left him always with a raging thirst. Hui Yuan was a famous monk from East Chin.

Two poems in tandem: feelings (1)

Honesty and folly are allotted by heaven;
adversity teaches us the ways of the world.
I lock my gate, receive no guests,
strain some wine and drink it with the wife.
Human traffic is scarce on the moss covered path;
the pine grove is void of the song of birds.
Plans to return to the country are deferred;
I am ashamed before T'ao Yuan-ming of Chin.

Sung impromptu

Without wine I stop singing;
without song I'm averse to wine.
I delight in both wine and song;
they go together, they complement each other.
I trust my hand to compose a verse;
I trust my mouth to drink a cup.
Ah, what is an incorrigible old man to do;
I've learned to enjoy both wine and song?
Wine never meant drinking a lot;
I couldn't keep up with a thousand songs.
Sitting face to face with a cup of wine brought on the mood;
I have no idea why this should be so.
As a result my sickness has grown progressively worse;
only with death will the habit be broken.
Thus it's not just me who gets upset;
those around me continually rebuke me.

Upon hearing that several county magistrates
have been dealing in stolen goods: two poems (1)

The harvest is bad; the people are all dying;
all that remains is skin and bone.
How much flesh is left on their bodies
that you want to shave off the last ounce?

Upon hearing that several county magistrates
have been dealing in stolen goods: two poems (2)

You've seen it, too, I presume:
    a groundhog drinking river water.
Drink all it likes, the most it can do is fill its belly.
I ask you: how many mouths do you have
that you covet the last scrap of flesh of the people?

Don't say administering a district is a joy: (1)

Don't say administering a district is a joy;
on the contrary administration is nothing but headaches.
The magistrate's office is noisy as the market place;
litigation files are piled high as a hill.
How can I impose taxes on a poor village?
It's painful to look at the prisoners that fill the jail.
No smile cracks my lips;
when will I be able to really enjoy myself?

Don't say administering a district is a joy: (2)

Don't say administering a district is a joy;
on the contrary administration brings new headaches.
I must rebuke subordinates with an angry face
while bending the knee and bowing to superiors.
Every spring I must look over the counties in my jurisdiction:
I must offer frequent rain rituals to the spirits.
There's never the slightest respite;
how can I think of absenting myself?

Drinking with friends:
a monk comes and asks for a poem

Intent on blotting out the world, we drank a thousand cups,
our exchanges warm and intimate in the lamplight.
Busy drinking, busy talking, we had no time for anything else:
suddenly a monk came and asked for a poem.

Walking slowly up and down waiting for someone

In the evening after the rain has cleared
        I walk up and down the green grass.
A crow flashes in flight in the setting sun.
The dog barks; I wonder have you come.
All I hear is the song of a tipsy traveller
        in front of the gate.

Song to the moon,
sung on the bank of the lotus pond

The lovely lady in the moon, prettying up
for a gathering of the Immortals in heaven,
suddenly annoyed by the dust occluding her mirror,
has come down to wash it in flowing blue waters.

To my son Sambaek on drinking wine (1)

Still of an age to be on the breast
    and already you're tilting the cup.
I fear before many years have gone,
    you'll surely rot your gut.
Don't learn an old man's crooked binges;
all your life people will say you're mad.

To my son Sambaek on drinking wine (2)

Every disaster in my life has been wine's doing;
how come already you love to drink?
I regret giving you the name Sambaek;
I fear you'll tilt three hundred cups a day.

Note: Sambaek literally means three hundred.

An old kisaeng

Face once lovely, now a flower fallen branch;
who can see the alluring fifteen-year-old you once were?
Song and dance are as beguiling as of old.
I am touched: your skills have not faded at all.

On poetry

Writing poetry is a consummate art:
expression and thought form a lovely harmony.
When thought's significance is truly deep
the flavor improves with every chew.
Deep thought without smooth expression
makes for coarse texture;
        the unfolding of meaning is precluded.
Decorating and chiselling for embellishment
are of secondary importance,
and yet it takes a supreme effort
to reject a fine line not quite to the point.
To grab the flower and abandon the fruit
causes the poem to lose real meaning.
Today's crop of poets ignore
the profound worth of the Book of Songs.
They decorate the skin colorfully;
they follow the fashion of the moment.
Meaning is postulated in Heaven;
it is hard to get it right.
Aware of this difficulty
they are content to decorate the exterior.
Thus they try to dazzle the crowd,
to conceal the absence of deep thought.
With the gradual development of this trend
good writing has been knocked to the ground.
Li Po and Tu Fu are not coming back;
on whose authority am I to sort
        the true from the false?
I want to repair the broken base of letters,

but there's no one to carry a basket of earth.
I can recite three hundred verses
        from the Book of Songs;
whom can I satirize, whom can I help?
All I can do is do what I can.
I cry alone: others laugh me to scorn.

Composed with springs flowing on all sides

Water gushes all around my house;
reed pipe and bamboo flute ring out everywhere.
Sitting here surrounded by the music of the Immortals,
it's as if I were in paradise.

The year of Imsul, winter, twelfth month,
went east with army H.Q. to obliterate the enemy:
presented to a guest who encouraged us
while drinking in Heavenly Life Temple

All my life I wouldn't put a finger on a grasshopper;
today I set out to pull the molars of a tigress.
When I sit at the royal banquet
        after the rebel army has been put down,
the king will pin the victory laurel in my hair.

At the entrance to Heavenly Life Temple

The green of the grass curls like smoke to the sky;
pear blossoms cover the ground like white snow.
This is the spot of our annual goodbyes;
I send no guest away today, yet my heart
dissolves in tears.

Child abandoned on the road (1)

Tigers and wolves though fierce
    never harm their young.
Has some woman abandoned
    her child on the road?
It's been quite a good year;
    there's no shortage of food.
It must be some woman newly wed
    who wants to impress her husband.

Child abandoned on the road (2)

Though the year, it's said, was not too good,
    and there's some hunger around,
no matter how much a child eats,
    how many spoons will it consume?
Can a mother and child
    become enemies in a morning?
Now I know how cruel
    human nature has become.

Cicada

Cicada, glad seeker of cool shade in the verdant forest,
so small your body, so resonant your cry.
Unaware that the lonely traveller bowed in care is listening,
you move from forest to forest crying the live long day.

Letting a rat go free

People steal everything under Heaven;
you steal what people stole.
Stratagems solely for mouth and belly:
why single you out for blame?

Presented to a kisaeng at a drinking party
after an illness

Wine has me dancing and singing for joy;
medicine makes my sick body fly.
Who unfolds the glory of spring again in an old man's eyes?
A kisaeng with jade face smiles a gracious smile.

Visited a friend in the snow
but did not meet him

The snow shines whiter than paper;
I take my whip and write my name and *cha*.
Don't let the wind sweep the spot;
kindly wait for the master to come.

Note: *Cha* is a name used in boyhood and retained by close friends afterwards.

Inconsequences: self-directed

The banks of Black Rock Stream are fine for evading heat;
the upper deck of Kaewon Pavilion is good for chanting poems.
The problem: official business encroaches so,
it's difficult to tip a cup even once a week.

View from my straw hut

My cute daughter chases a butterfly: the butterfly flutters;
my little son catches a cicada: the cicada buzzes frantically.
I read a bit, doze a bit, try to read what's left;
the words drift gradually to slurred somniloquence.

CORNELL EAST ASIA SERIES

For ordering information, please contact the Cornell East Asia Series, East Asia Program, Cornell University, 140 Uris Hall, Ithaca, NY 14853-7601, USA; phone (607) 255-6222, fax (607) 255-1388, e-mail kks3@cornell.edu.

Singing Like a Cricket, Hooting Like an Owl

Yi Kyu-bo (1168-1241), the greatest of the classical Korean poets, was born into a very turbulent period of history, when the Koryô kingdom was threatened from the north by barbarians and from within by the ongoing struggle for supremacy among the various factions. His poems, confessional and transcendent, describe moments of personal illumination in the course of everyday life.

KEVIN O'ROURKE is professor of English at Kyunghee University, Seoul. His translations include *Ten Korean Short Stories; Our Twisted Hero; The Shijo Tradition;* and *Tilting the Jar, Spilling the Moon,* which was the Poetry Society translation selection for 1993.

9-95/.5M paper/.2M cloth/TS